Whales and Dolphins

Anita Ganeri

KINGFISHER

NEW YORK

KINGFISHER
LONDON & NEW YORK

Copyright © Kingfisher 2013
Published in the United States by Kingfisher,
175 Fifth Ave., New York, NY 10010
Kingfisher is an imprint of
Macmillan Children's Books, London.
All rights reserved.

Distributed in the U.S. by Macmillan,
175 Fifth Ave., New York, NY 10010

Illustrations by Peter Bull Art Studio

Library of Congress Cataloging-in-Publication data
has been applied for.

ISBN: 978-0-7534-6815-9

Kingfisher books are available for special promotions
and premiums. For details contact: Special Markets
Department, Macmillan, 175 Fifth Ave.,
New York, NY 10010.

For more information, please visit
www.kingfisherbooks.com

Printed in China
1 3 5 7 9 8 6 4 2
1TR/0313/UTD/WKT/140MA

Picture credits

**The Publisher would like to thank the following
for permission to reproduce their material.
(t = top, b = bottom, c = center, l = left, r = right):**
Pages 4–5 Frank Lane Picture Agency (FLPA)/Flip Nicklin/
Minden; 4br Naturepl/Jeff Rotman; 5cl Naturepl/Gabriel Rojo;
6 Getty/Paul Nicklin/NGS; 8tr Shutterstock/idreamphoto; 8b
Naturepl/Mark Carwardine; 9tr FLPA/Jean-Pierre Sylvestre/
Bios; 9cl Shutterstock/Tatiana Ivkovich; 9c Getty/OSF; 9br Getty/
Mark Carwardine; 10 Shutterstock/CampCrazy Photography;
12tl FLPA/Norbert Wu/Minden; 12cr Naturepl/David Tipling; 13tl
Getty/Brian J. Skerry/NGS; 13cr FLPA/Bios; 13bl AWL/Images/
Danita Delimont; 13br Seapics/Doug Perrine; 14 Alamy/Danita
Delimont; 16–17 FLPA/Flip Nicklin/Minden; 16cl FLPA/Flip Nicklin/
Minden; 16bl Alamy/WaterFrame; 16br FLPA/Flip Nicklin/Minden;
17tr Naturepl/Alex Mustard; 17br Naturepl/Brandon Cole; 18
FLPA/Newman; 20cl FLPA/Bios; 20b FLPA/Bios; 21tl FLPA/
Reinhard Dirschel; 21tr FLPA/Flip Nicklin/Minden; 21b Naturepl/
Todd Pusser; 22 Alamy/Kevin Schafer; 24tr Corbis/Isabel
Beasley/Reuters; 24b Corbis/Chor Sokunthea/Reuters; 25tr
Reuters/Andres Stapff; 25cl Reuters/Janghir Khan; 25cr Ardea/
Mark Carwardine; 25bl Seapics/Roland Seitre; 25br Corbis/
Christine Osborne; 26 SeaPics/Phillip Colla; 28cl Getty/Barcroft
Media; 28cr FLPA/Flip Nicklin/Minden; 28bl Corbis/Jeff Rotman;
28br Corbis/Tony Arruza; 29tr Getty/AFP Photo/Greg Wood;
29b Corbis/Ocean; 30tl Alamy/Steven J. Kazlowski; 30tr FLPA/
Flip Nicklin/Minden; 30ctl Nature/Sue Flood; 30ctr Nature/Mark
Carwardine; 30cbr Corbis/Michael Nicholson; 30bl Nature/Todd
Pusser; 31tr Nature/Mark Carwardine; 31cl Alamy/AF Archive;
31ctr FLPA/Frans Lanting; 31bl Specialist Stock/M. Lane/
WILDLIFE; 31br Shutterstock/idreamphoto.

Contents

More to explore

On some of the pages in this book, you will find colored buttons with symbols on them. There are four different colors, and each belongs to a different topic. Choose a topic, follow its colored buttons through the book, and you'll make some interesting discoveries of your own.

For example, on page 6 you'll find a green button, like this, next to a polar scene. The green buttons are about places where whales and dolphins live.

Page 27

Environment

There is a page number in the button. Turn to that page (page 27) to find a green button on another whale habitat. Follow all the steps through the book, and at the end of your journey you'll find out how the steps are linked and discover even more information about this topic.

Record breakers

Whale stories

Communication

The other topics in this book are record breakers, whale stories, and communication. Follow the steps and see what you can discover!

The whale family

Whales are mammals that live in the sea. The whale family also includes dolphins and porpoises. There are around 80 types. Like humans, they are warm-blooded and breathe air. They come to the surface to breathe.

Scientists study a blue whale from their boat

a bottlenose dolphin calf with its mother

Baby dolphins, whales, and porpoises are taken care of by their mothers and fed milk. They stay with their moms for two to three years. A young whale is called a calf.

The blue whale is the biggest animal that has ever lived. It can grow up to 100 ft. (30m) long and weigh as much as 35 elephants. The water helps support its huge bulk.

blue whale

sperm whale

Whales are the largest members of the whale family. Some—such as blue, humpback, and sperm whales—are called "great whales" because of their size.

Whales look smooth, but like all mammals they have some hair.

whiskers around a right whale's mouth

vaquita porpoise

Porpoises are the smallest members of the whale family, around 7 ft. (2m) long or less. They have blunter, rounder heads than dolphins and no beaks.

Dolphins are 6–10 ft. (2–3m) long. They have long, pointed snouts called beaks. They are fast swimmers and are often very acrobatic.

white-beaked dolphin

Ocean home

Whales and dolphins live in oceans around the world—from warm, tropical waters to icy, polar seas. They swim, feed, breed, and play in their ocean home. Some travel huge distances across the sea to feed and breed.

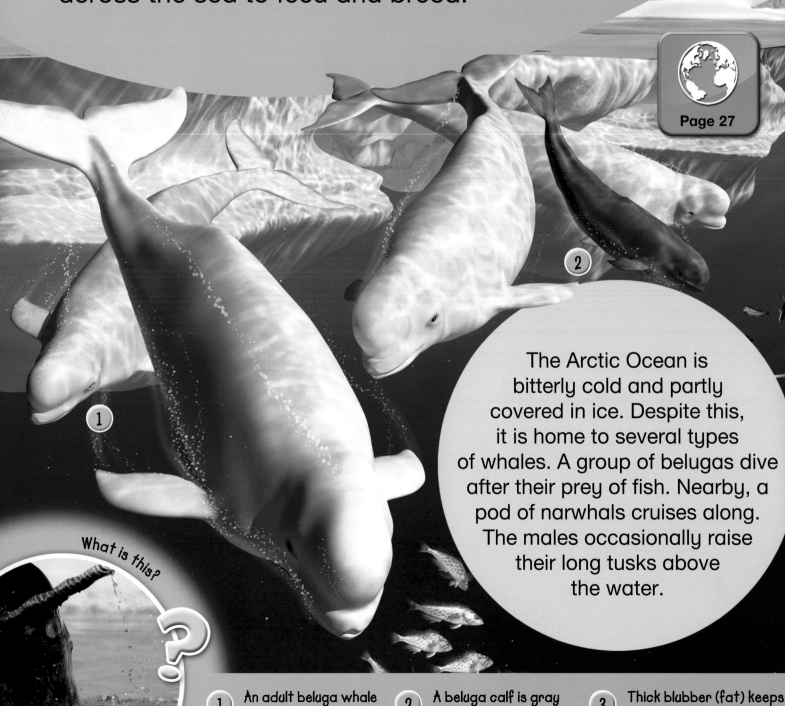

Page 27

The Arctic Ocean is bitterly cold and partly covered in ice. Despite this, it is home to several types of whales. A group of belugas dive after their prey of fish. Nearby, a pod of narwhals cruises along. The males occasionally raise their long tusks above the water.

What is this?

1 An adult beluga whale has white skin.

2 A beluga calf is gray but turns white later on.

3 Thick blubber (fat) keeps this bowhead whale war

? This is a male narwhal's long tusk. It can grow up to 10 ft. (3m) long.

4

3

5

Page 18

Page 26

6

4 Seabirds soar over the ocean looking for fish.

5 A male narwhal has a long upper tooth called a tusk.

6 A female narwhal does not have a tusk.

Life in the sea

Whales and dolphins are perfectly adapted for life in the water. Their bodies are streamlined for swimming, with flippers for turning and balancing. They come to the surface to breathe air through small openings called blowholes.

dorsal (back) fin

This **dwarf minke whale** has a typical whale's body. Under its skin, it has a thick layer of fat called blubber. This helps keep the whale warm in the sea.

blowhole

Minke whales live in seas around the world.

flipper

This **tail** belongs to a humpback whale. It has two parts, called flukes. Whales move their tails up and down to power their bodies through the water.

A right whale leaps out of the water. This is called breaching.

dorsal fin

finless porpoise

A single blowhole is found in toothed whales, such as sperm whales, orcas, dolphins, and porpoises. As the animal breathes out, its "blow" looks like a jet of steam.

sei whale

The pointed **dorsal (back) fin** of an orca sticks up above the water. The fin can grow up to 6 ft. (1.8m) high—as tall as an adult human.

Double blowholes are found in baleen whales, such as fin, blue, and sei whales. The two holes are side by side on the top of the head. Air goes in and out of the whale's body through its blowholes.

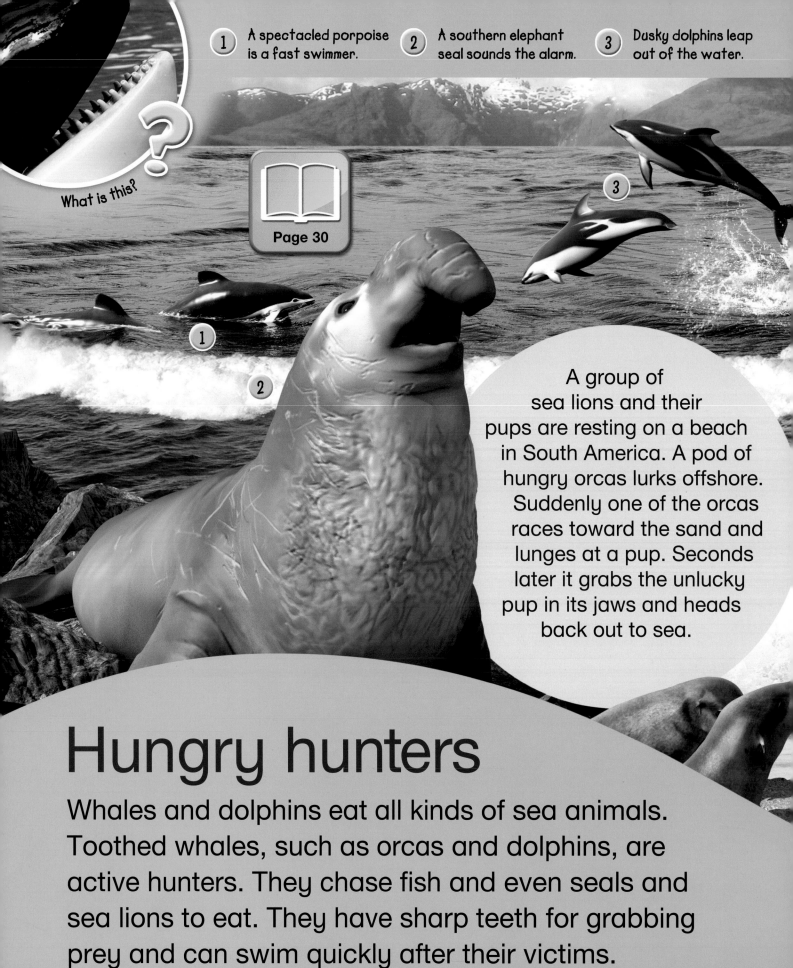

1 A spectacled porpoise is a fast swimmer.

2 A southern elephant seal sounds the alarm.

3 Dusky dolphins leap out of the water.

What is this?

Page 30

A group of sea lions and their pups are resting on a beach in South America. A pod of hungry orcas lurks offshore. Suddenly one of the orcas races toward the sand and lunges at a pup. Seconds later it grabs the unlucky pup in its jaws and heads back out to sea.

Hungry hunters

Whales and dolphins eat all kinds of sea animals. Toothed whales, such as orcas and dolphins, are active hunters. They chase fish and even seals and sea lions to eat. They have sharp teeth for grabbing prey and can swim quickly after their victims.

4

Page 15

Page 15

5

6

This is a close-up of an orca's teeth. They are large and nail-like for grabbing prey.

Dolphins also use echolocation to find their way around.

Dolphins use **echolocation** to find their prey. They make clicking sounds that hit objects in the water and send back echoes. The dolphins listen for the echoes to figure out where there are fish to eat.

Blue whales eat tons of tiny shrimp called krill.

krill

Food and feeding

Toothed whales, such as orcas and dolphins, use their teeth for grabbing prey. Baleen whales, such as blue and humpback whales, have bristly brushes (baleen) inside their mouths instead of teeth. They use their baleen to sift tiny creatures out of the sea.

baleen

A baleen whale swims along with its mouth open. It gulps in water and then pushes it out again through its baleen. The baleen works like a strainer, trapping any food.

A dolphin's teeth are wide and cone-shaped for catching slippery prey, such as fish and squid. They are the same shape all along its jaw. A dolphin has between 60 and 100 teeth.

pointed teeth

humpback whales feeding

Bubble "nets" are used by humpback whales to trap food. The whales blow bubbles around a school of fish or krill. Then they swim up through the middle with their mouths wide open.

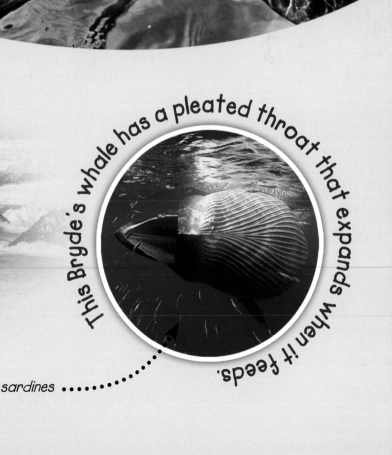

This Bryde's whale has a pleated throat that expands when it feeds.

sardines

1 A sperm whale breaches (leaps out of the water).

2 A female sperm whale is giving birth.

3 The calf is born tail first.

What is this?

Page 10

Birth of a whale

A baby whale, or calf, is born underwater, usually tail first. Its mother nudges it gently toward the surface so that it can take its first breath. The calf is able to swim straightaway. Most whales have one calf at a time—twins are very rare.

Page 22

It is breeding time for these sperm whales. A group of females and their young swims through the ocean. Some of the females are mothers with calves. Others are "aunts" who help take care of the calves while their mothers go and find food. A whale calf stays with its mom for two to three years, feeding on her milk.

Page 30

This is a sperm whale's wrinkly skin.

Family life

Many whales and dolphins live in family groups called pods or schools. There may be tens or even hundreds of animals in a group. They help each other find food and take care of young. They have special ways of talking to each other underwater.

Male narwhals use their long tusks for jousting during the breeding season. They fight to win over females and to establish their position in the pod.

Male humpback whales hang in the water and sing songs to attract females. Each song can last for around half an hour, and the male may sing it over and over again.

A fin whale has the loudest voice of any whale.

Atlantic spotted dolphins live in close, strongly bonded pods made up of males, females, and young. The pod members feed and swim together, staying close if there is danger in the area.

Older animals are covered in light and dark spots.

A bottlenose whale mother swims with her calf. Young bottlenose whales are usually much darker in color than their parents.

Belugas are nicknamed "sea canaries" because they whistle and chirp like birds. They also click and squeak. They use these sounds to communicate with other members of the pod.

A long journey

Every year many whales make long journeys across the sea to find the best places to feed and breed. This is called migration. The whales swim in groups, occasionally spyhopping—lifting their heads above water to look around.

Page 11

What are these?

① A gray whale dives for food.

② Anchovies are the whales' prey.

③ Hungry orcas lurk nearby.

? These are barnacles (a type of shellfish) on a gray whale's back.

3

4

Page 30

A group of gray whales is nearing the end of its migration. The whales have swum from their feeding grounds in the Arctic Ocean to their breeding grounds off the coast of Mexico—a distance of around 6,200 mi. (10,000km). A pod of orcas waits, ready to prey on the weak or sick.

5

6

Page 30

4 A gray whale spyhops to look around.

5 The leatherback turtle is the largest sea turtle.

6 A manta ray has winglike fins.

On the move

A whale or dolphin's body is streamlined for swimming. The animal powers through the water in smooth, arching movements with the help of its muscular tail. As the tail moves up and down, it propels the whale's body forward.

Whales rest by "logging" –hanging still in the water.

A Dall's porpoise does everything at high speed, even surfacing to breathe. In rough seas a spray of water appears from its head and along its back. This is known as a rooster tail.

a humpback whale logging

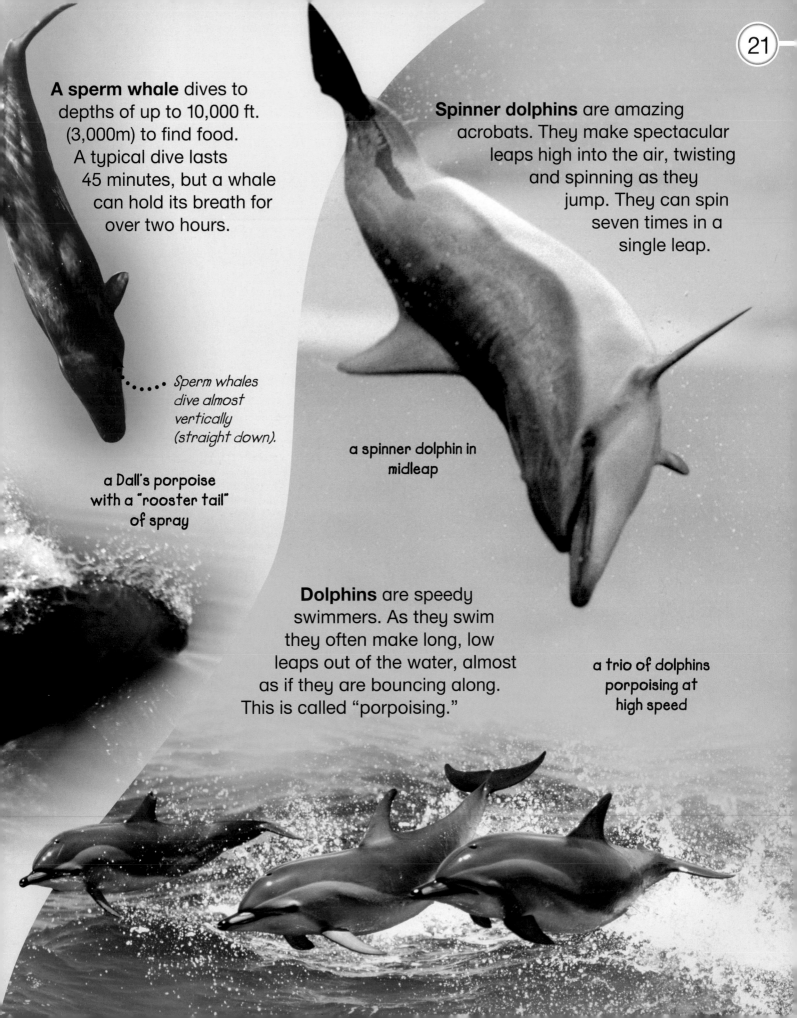

A sperm whale dives to depths of up to 10,000 ft. (3,000m) to find food. A typical dive lasts 45 minutes, but a whale can hold its breath for over two hours.

Sperm whales dive almost vertically (straight down).

a Dall's porpoise with a "rooster tail" of spray

Spinner dolphins are amazing acrobats. They make spectacular leaps high into the air, twisting and spinning as they jump. They can spin seven times in a single leap.

a spinner dolphin in midleap

Dolphins are speedy swimmers. As they swim they often make long, low leaps out of the water, almost as if they are bouncing along. This is called "porpoising."

a trio of dolphins porpoising at high speed

In the river

Several types of dolphins live in rivers and lakes. They are specifically adapted to their homes. Most are almost blind, since eyes are useless in the murky water. Instead, like their seagoing cousins, the dolphins use echolocation (see page 12) to find their way.

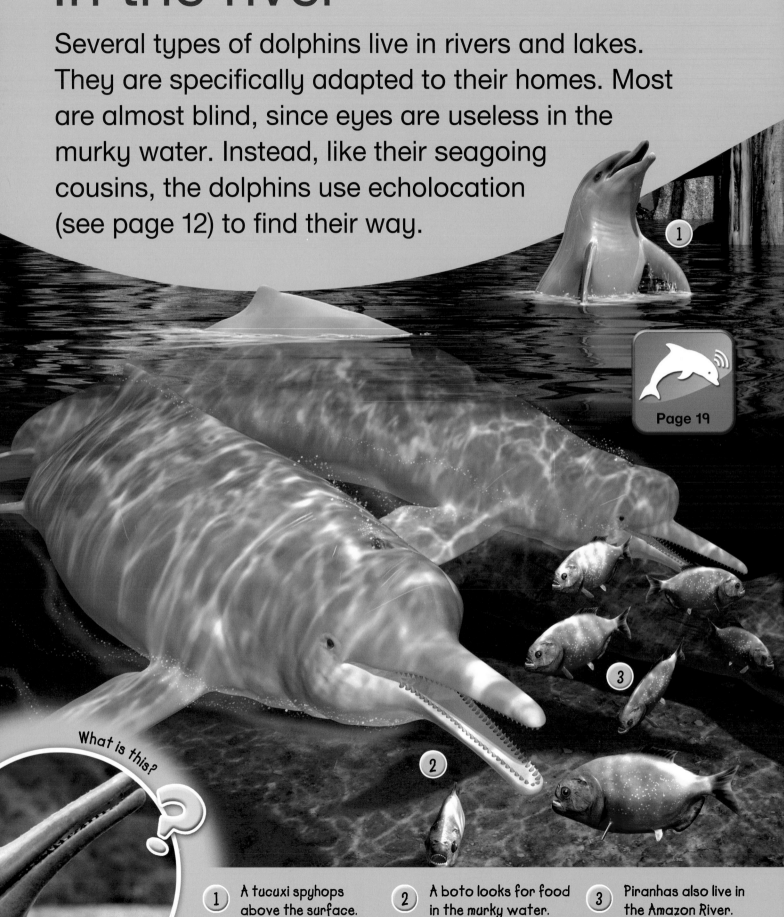

Page 19

What is this?

1. A tucuxi spyhops above the surface.

2. A boto looks for food in the murky water.

3. Piranhas also live in the Amazon River.

? This is a boto's long beak. It is full of small, pointed teeth for catching fish.

5

Page 19

4

6

It is early evening on a muddy stretch of the Amazon River in South America. A group of botos has come out to feed. These long-beaked river dolphins share their home with giant otters, piranha fish, and tucuxis—another type of dolphin.

4 A boto rests on its side with its flipper in the air.

5 Sleek giant otters hunt fish in the river.

6 Botos have a bulging forehead, or "melon."

River dolphins

Most river dolphins are very rare. They face many risks out in the wild. They may become trapped in fishing nets or be injured by boats' propellers. Their main threat, though, is pollution. Some river dolphins are also hunted by people for food.

The Irrawaddy dolphin is found in rivers in southeast Asia, where it can swim over 600 mi. (1,000km) upstream. It also lives in shallow, sheltered coastal waters.

The snubfin dolphin lives off the northern coast of Australia. It was named as a new species in 2005. Before this scientists believed it was a type of Irrawaddy dolphin.

an Irrawaddy dolphin peeking above the surface

This baby **La Plata dolphin** was lucky to be rescued. It had become tangled in a fishing net. Many dolphins die in this way because they cannot reach the surface to breathe.

The Yangtze River dolphin was declared extinct in 2006. It was only found in the Yangtze River, China, one of the busiest and dirtiest rivers in the world.

▲ Ganges River dolphin sticks its head out of the water.

Females have longer beaks than males.

Dams built across rivers cause problems for dolphins. They block the flow of the river and the dolphins cannot travel to find food or mates.

This **Indus River dolphin** was rescued from an irrigation canal (built to carry river water to farmers' fields). Stuck there, it would not have been able to find food to eat.

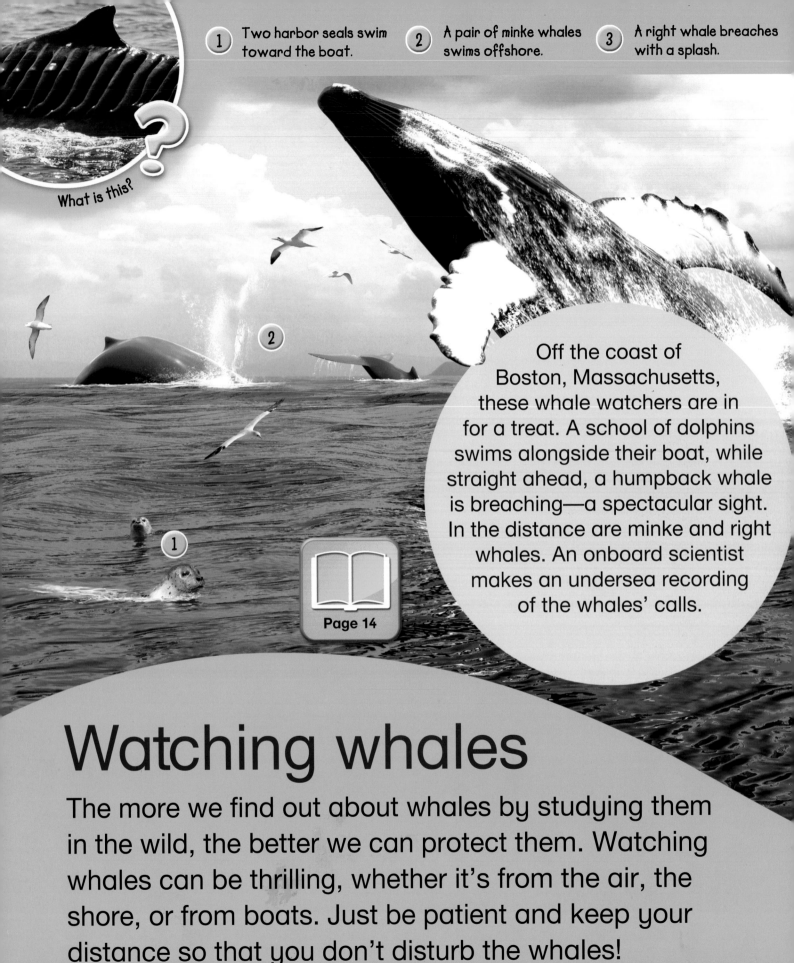

Page 14

1 Two harbor seals swim toward the boat.

2 A pair of minke whales swims offshore.

3 A right whale breaches with a splash.

What is this?

Off the coast of Boston, Massachusetts, these whale watchers are in for a treat. A school of dolphins swims alongside their boat, while straight ahead, a humpback whale is breaching—a spectacular sight. In the distance are minke and right whales. An onboard scientist makes an undersea recording of the whales' calls.

Watching whales

The more we find out about whales by studying them in the wild, the better we can protect them. Watching whales can be thrilling, whether it's from the air, the shore, or from boats. Just be patient and keep your distance so that you don't disturb the whales!

4 Another whale-watching boat stops nearby.

5 White-sided dolphins leap above the waves.

6 A scientist prepares to throw recording equipment into the sea.

27

Page 23

? These are scars on a humpback whale's body made by a boat propeller.

Saving whales

Around the world, whales and dolphins face many threats. They are hunted, caught in fishing nets, and harmed by litter and pollution in the sea. Scientists and conservationists work hard to study these amazing animals and to protect them.

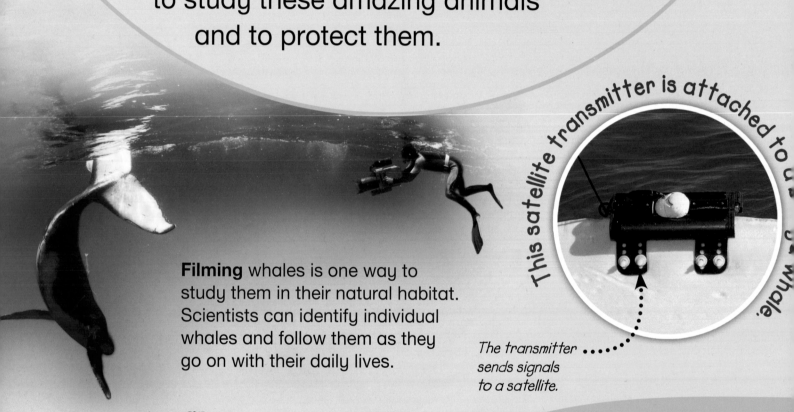

Filming whales is one way to study them in their natural habitat. Scientists can identify individual whales and follow them as they go on with their daily lives.

This satellite transmitter is attached to us of whale.

The transmitter sends signals to a satellite.

In some places, people can swim with dolphins.

Whaling means hunting whales for their meat and other products. This old carving shows a whaling ship. Today most whaling is banned.

Saving whales that are stranded is a difficult task. Here volunteers in Australia pour water over beached false killer whales to keep them wet and cool until they can be refloated.

Whales can become stranded if they hunt too close to shore.

Fishing nets can be deadly to whales and dolphins. If they get trapped in one, they cannot come to the surface to breathe and may drown. Around 1,000 die in this way every day.

Record breakers

Bowhead whales have the longest baleen plates of any whale. They can be over 13 ft. (4m) long. When the whale's mouth is closed, its bottom jaw covers the baleen.

...... *baleen*

Gray whales make the longest migration of any whale or any mammal. Their yearly journey from Mexico to the Arctic and back again is around 12,500 mi. (20,000km) long.

Environment

The beluga is perfectly adapted to its **Arctic Ocean** home. It is able to locate the rare air spaces under the ice, and its white skin helps camouflage it.

Watching whales in their **natural habitat** is becoming more popular. But it is vital that any money made is used to help protect the whales and their environment.

whale spyhopping ....

Whale stories

narwhal's tusk

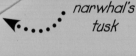

The legendary **unicorn's** spiral horn is based on the narwhal's tusk. In reality there is nothing magical about the tusk—it is just a very long top tooth.

The Bible tells the tale of **Jonah,** who is saved from drowning when a whale swallows him. Jonah spends three days and nights in the whale.

Communication

Orcas use **whistles, clicks,** and other sounds to stay in touch with the other members of their pod while they are swimming or hunting. Each pod has its own set of sounds.

Sperm whales use **patterns of clicks** to communicate. Each whale has a different pattern. Baby whales have to learn how to "speak," just like human babies do.

More to explore

Orcas are the fastest-swimming whales. They can reach a top speed of 35 mph (55km/h)—six times faster than the quickest human swimmer.

orcas speeding along the surface

Sperm whales have the largest heads and the largest brains of any animal. A sperm whale brain weighs almost 17 lb. (8kg)—that's five times as much as a human's brain.

The tucuxi is at home in **salt and freshwater** habitats. It lives in the Amazon River and around the edges of the southern Atlantic. It feeds on catfish, small crabs, and shrimp.

Gray whales breed in warm, sheltered **bays and lagoons** along the coast of Mexico. The shallow water helps protect the babies from shark attacks.

gray whale ·······
calf

white sperm whale

Moby Dick is a story of a whaling ship trying to track down a ferocious white sperm whale. The book was based on sightings of an actual whale in the early 1800s.

The **Haida people** of North America believe that orcas are the most powerful animals in the sea. They tell stories of orcas that live in amazing underwater cities.

Haida carving

Echolocation allows dolphins to build up a sound picture of their surroundings. In murky river water, this ability is much more useful than having good eyesight.

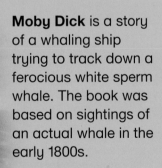

····· boto river dolphin

Breaching is when a whale or dolphin launches itself into the air and then falls back into the water with a great big splash. This may be a way of sending signals, or it may just be for fun.

Index